ReGroup™

training **groups** to be **groups**

Participant's Guide

Henry **Cloud**, Bill **Donahue**,
and John **Townsend**

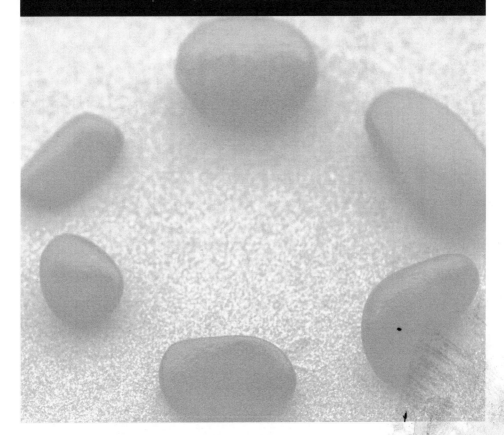

ReGroup™
training **groups** to be **groups**

Participant's Guide

Henry **Cloud**, Bill **Donahue**,
and John **Townsend**

ZONDERVAN®   groupware™   WILLOW

We want to hear from you. Please send your comments about this book to us in care of zreview@zondervan.com. Thank you

ZONDERVAN®

ReGroup™ Participant's Guide
Copyright 2007 by Willow Creek Association, Henry Cloud, and John Townsend

Requests for information should be addressed to:
Zondervan, *Grand Rapids, Michigan 49530*

ISBN-10: 0-310-27785-X
ISBN-13: 978-0-310-27785-9

Published in association with Yates & Yates, LLP, Attorneys and Counselors, Orange California.

Interior design by Blum Graphic Design

Printed in the United States of America

07 08 09 10 11 12 13 • 20 19 18 17 16 15 14 13 12 11 10 9 8 7 6 5 4 3 2 1

dedication

To all those who are seeking community, growth, and the life of God through small groups. May God bless you.

table of | Contents

A few years ago, a small gathering of group-minded folks met to discuss the training of group leaders. What could we do to make that training effective, accessible, and highly relevant? One answer was clear—that we should use a DVD format and show small group dramas that illustrated the teaching. As future discussions emerged and brainstorming sessions were completed, we had an "aha!" moment: why just train leaders when we can train entire groups?

Thanks to a ton of people, that idea has become a reality. Without these individuals, our idea for a product might still be sitting on a laptop or languishing dormant on our desks. It takes a team of highly skilled artists, writers, designers, video experts, drama writers, production geniuses, and actors to bring all this together.

Many thanks to Rex Minor, who shares our passion for spiritual formation through groups and who introduced Bill to Henry and John. Wendy Seidman, Christine Anderson, and Stephanie Oakley of the WCA helped us—no, actually forced us—to move beyond idealistic concepts to create actual learning experiences for groups that would be transferable and applicable to real life. In addition, Stephanie Oakley worked hard to develop the participant's guide, linking it with the DVD material.

The WCA Publishing Team of Nancy Raney, Christine Anderson, and Doug Yonamine worked hard with Sealy Yates, Cloud-Townsend Ministries, and Zondervan to guide the development of this unique project in a professional and honoring way. The marketing expertise of Greg Bowman and April Kimura-Anderson at the WCA helped develop a process that would get the word out in a creative way, relevant and applicable to all groups. Maureen Price of Cloud-Townsend Resources brought insight, inspiration, and creativity to the project.

Dave Schwartz of DAV Productions and the WCA Media Team provided creative and innovative production expertise in the filming of the DVDs. Jeff Berryman wrote and directed phenomenal scripts, and Steve Pederson brought together an incredible team of actors: Rod and Deanna Armentrout, Jasmin Cardenas, Tim Gregory, Blaine Hogan, Lucas Peterson, Faith Russell, and Lori Woodall.

The always amazing administrative support of Cindy Martucci, Janet Williams, Jaime Fontaine, and Stephanie Walsh helped Bill, John, Henry, and the WCA Content Development Team move forward with meetings and countless conference calls. The Marketing Team at Zondervan, along with John Raymond, Stan Gundry, and Scott Bolinder, helped get this product to market so that churches around the globe could benefit.

To all of these people—and probably a few dozen more who supported them—we are very grateful. Your God-given gifts and talents have been well stewarded, and the church will be forever impacted by your work.

introduction

Welcome to ReGroup™! You are about to embark on a revolutionary journey into what it means to be a safe, caring, and helpful small group community. ReGroup™ is a learning process, an environment where you will discover how to grow in faith as you build authentic relationships and accomplish the purpose for which you gathered.

The ReGroup™ material is designed for the whole group, not just the leader. As you all participate in creating a healthy group environment, everyone benefits. If you do not have a designated leader, ReGroup™ will provide the initial guidance and structure to help you form a meaningful group experience and move ahead. If you have an official leader, that person has already taken a level of responsibility to provide some guidance. But research shows successful groups work alongside their leaders and share responsibility for members' needs and the group's outcomes. So do your best to participate in the process of personal and group growth. The group needs you—and you need the group.

As a teaching and training tool, ReGroup™ is more than simply a series of lectures. It is designed to bring you the practical insights of Henry Cloud, Bill Donahue, and John Townsend by using training talks, creative dramas, and small group experiences which will guide you in becoming an effective group.

If this is your first group experience, this material will lead you one step at a time, helping you develop the relational environment in which groups thrive. If you have had other group experiences, chances are you need a refresher course—or maybe you were never exposed to some of these ideas. It is good to take a few meetings and make sure the whole group is on track—whether you are a newcomer or an experienced small group person.

Perhaps a few of you are skeptical because you had a poor group experience in the past—in church, at work, or with a volunteer organization. It might have been the leader, or the group process, or maybe the curriculum, or the members—or all of the above. No group is perfect. But in many cases, groups fail simply because no one ever helps them discover how to really be a group.

Learning to be an effective group is just as important as the material your group is studying. We believe that as you learn the skills and processes for developing a meaningful group experience, you will experience spiritual growth and be able to use your materials more effectively. Whether you are a Bible study, a prayer group, a ministry team, a work group, or a home group, ReGroup™ is designed to help you connect deeply, focus on your purpose, grow in life skills, and become a powerful community for transformation.

Getting Started

As you use DVD One, which guides your group through four complete group meetings, we will ask you to give us about an hour of your group time. In effect, we will be your group coaches. During that hour each meeting, you will learn the biblical purpose for your group, begin to build or strengthen relationships, establish your ground rules so your group functions authentically, and clarify your direction and goals so your group achieves the purpose for which you gathered. This is only for the first four meetings.

Then, building from that foundation, DVD Two will coach you to greater effectiveness as a community. There are 13 short coaching tips (about 5–10 minutes each) designed to help you practice an essential component of group life. Most include role plays and dramas to model a particular skill, such as active listening, learning to tell your story, effective prayer, balancing participation of members, confronting obstacles in your group, handling pain, and more. View one of these tips at the beginning of your meeting, and then practice using the new skill throughout the course of your meeting time, within the context of your regular study or discussion. At the end of the meeting, there is a short debrief time to review how it felt to use that skill in the group.

In addition, there are three extended coaching tips that cover challenging issues—confrontation, conflict, and dealing with a crisis. These tips will require an entire group meeting to work through and can be used as your group matures and encounters the realities of life.

Your participant guide is a tool to help you work as a team while you develop group values and build relationships with each other. It provides resources to help you in each group meeting, plus tools for further study and investigation in your personal life.

Get ready for a challenging and productive experience in community! If you are willing to work together—and expect to partner with your leader as an entire team—your group will become a powerful place for change, growth, and encouragement.

We wish you the best,
Henry, Bill, and John

Kevin and Faith Reese

Kevin and Faith colead the small group. They have three children, the youngest of which has recently suffered a stroke. Kevin manages an office, and Faith works as a freelance artist. Kevin is an old friend of Michael's, and Faith is friends with Leisha.

Gregory and Julie King

Gregory works as a carpenter, and Julie teaches third grade.

Marty Dillard

Marty works in a bookstore, but dreams of making it in Hollywood. He is engaged to Veronica.

Veronica Marquez

Veronica is engaged to Marty and works as a social worker.

Michael Tran

Michael is single. He works in an office, but is very handy and enjoys woodworking. He is a friend of Kevin's.

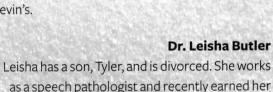

Dr. Leisha Butler

Leisha has a son, Tyler, and is divorced. She works as a speech pathologist and recently earned her doctorate. She and Faith are friends..

ReGroup
training **groups** to be **groups**

DVD one participant's guide

| getting connected—
God's purpose for
small groups

session one | getting connected—
God's purpose
for small
groups

Welcome to Regroup™! We are excited to begin the journey with you and your group. This resource is designed to be a training experience for both members and leaders, so the entire group can see, learn, and understand the essential elements for successful, growing small groups—together.

Please insert DVD One and select **"Session One: Getting Connected—God's Purpose for Small Groups"** to begin.

Watch this . . . 8 minutes
"Segment One: Why Groups?"

getting connected—
God's purpose for
small groups

Talk about this . . . 12 minutes

Go around the group and share the following:

- My name is . . . (if the group is new)

- What impacted me the most about the interviews was . . .

When everyone has shared, select *"Segment Two: God's Purpose for Groups"* from the Session One menu.

| # getting connected—God's purpose for small groups

Watch this . . . 12 minutes

"Segment Two: God's Purpose for Groups"

- The "theology" of small groups: God uses people to bring grace and transformation

  - ▶ Ephesians 4:16—"From him the whole body, joined and held together by every supporting ligament, grows and builds itself up in love, as each part does its work."
  - ▶ I Peter 4:10—"Each one should use whatever gift he has received to serve others, faithfully administering God's grace in its various forms."
  - ▶ John 17:20–21—Jesus desires for us to experience oneness and unity

- The goal of small groups is spiritual growth

- Grace, truth, and time

  - ▶ Grace: God is for you
  - ▶ Truth: reality that comes from Scripture and other people
  - ▶ Time: the process by which growth and transformation occur

getting connected—
God's purpose for
small groups

 Talk about this . . . 25 minutes

To the degree they feel comfortable, have each person share their answer to the following question:

- Pick one word from the list below you would use to describe your current connection or relationship with God and explain why you chose that word. You can use a word that is not on the list if you want to.

Close	New	Careful
Disconnected	Intimidating	Boring
Searching	Unsure	Alone
Friendly	Loving	Questioning
Open	Safe	Nonexistent
Angry	Strange	Peaceful
Mysterious	Doubtful	Overwhelming
Afraid	Life-giving	Stagnant
Dynamic	In trouble	Other: _____

When everyone has shared, select
"Segment Three: Closing Thoughts"
from the Session One menu.

| getting connected—
God's purpose for
small groups

 Watch this . . . 3 minutes
"Segment Three: Closing Thoughts"

What we've covered . . .

- Groups are God's delivery system of care: he uses people

- The outcome of group life is spiritual growth in all areas of life

- "Oneness" is God's desire for his people

Coming up . . .
Discovering the five habits of a successful group

Close the group in prayer.

session two | five habits of life-changing groups

session two |
five habits of life-changing groups

Welcome back! Please insert DVD One and select **"Session Two: Five Habits of Life-Changing Groups"** to begin.

Watch this . . . 23 minutes

"Segment One: The Five Essential Habits"

- Review: grace, truth, and time

- The five essential habits

 Drama: Violating the Five Habits

Five habits that create a grace-filled, truth-telling group:

Care
- Being "for" each other
- Encouraging each other
- Coming alongside one another

Safety
- Having a "come-as-you-are" culture
- Feeling safe enough to be yourself
- Accepting each other unconditionally

Authenticity
- Being "real" with each other
- Taking relational risks with one another

Growth
- Hebrews 10:24—spurring one another on
- Pushing each other to take growth steps
- Naming areas where growth needs to happen

Help
- Providing resources others may need
- Can be practical: helping move, filing tax returns, etc.
- It's also about asking for help when it's needed

Turn the page to begin filling out the chart
as you watch the drama.

| five habits of life-changing groups

Drama: Using the Five Habits

As you watch the drama, look and listen for how group members use the five habits. Below is a chart with the group members' names and each of the habits. If you see a habit being used by a character, make a check in the appropriate box. (To see the answers, turn to page 141.)

	Care	Safety	Authen-ticity	Growth	Help
Kevin					
Faith					
Michael					
Marty					
Veronica					
Gregory					
Julie					
Leisha					

Talk about this . . . 35 minutes

Part 1: (25 minutes)

- Share with the group the one habit that most resonated with you or is most important to you and why. Practice "authenticity" (being real) as you share.

- The rest of the group should practice "safety" while listening. This means no judgment and no condemnation; let the person who shared know that they are safe and accepted.

- Continue with the exercise until everyone has had a chance to share.

When everyone has shared, please turn the page to continue the activity.

 Talk about this . . . (cont'd)

Part 2: (10 minutes)

Now talk honestly about how the discussion went:

- When you were talking, were you able to be authentic (real)? Why or why not?

- When you were listening, did the group environment feel safe? Why or why not?

When everyone has shared, select
"Segment Two: Closing Thoughts" from the
Session Two menu.

Watch this ... 2 minutes
"Segment Two: Closing Thoughts"

What we've covered ...
- Groups need to be grace-filled and truth- telling

- The five core habits of a small group

Coming up ...
- Determining your group's "ground rules"

Close the group in prayer.

session three | setting ground rules

session three | setting ground rules

Welcome back! Please insert DVD One and select **"Session Three: Setting Ground Rules"** to begin.

Watch this . . . 22 minutes
"Segment One: What Are Ground Rules?"

- Ground rules provide the "guard rails" for a group

  ▶ Clear expectations are essential for a good outcome
  ▶ Ground rules ensure that the five habits flourish in the group

- The role of the leader

  ▶ Responsible for making sure the ground rules work
  ▶ Stewards the process and purpose of the group

Definition:
Ground rules are rules agreed upon by all members of the group that ensure the group process works.

Examples of ground rules:

- Begin and end on time
- Attend the meetings!
- Call when you can't come
- Appoint a timekeeper

Others:

- No interrupting or carrying on separate conversations
- Participation
- Confidentiality / safety
- Bring up issues or dissatisfaction right away
- Leave the group well

 Drama: Broken Ground Rules

Turn the page to list the ground rules you saw
broken in the drama.

session three | setting ground rules

 **Do this . . .**

Discuss together what ground rules you saw broken in the drama and list them below. Feel free to review the drama again. (To see the answers, turn to page 141.)

Broken ground rules:

_____

_____

_____

_____

_____

_____

_____

_____

_____

 Resume DVD

Things to keep in mind:
- Comfortable environment
- Food—keep it simple!
- Childcare considerations

 Talk about this . . . 20 minutes

- For the next 20 minutes, come up with your group's "ground rules." We've already included a few we think are foundational and left space to brainstorm your own on the next page.

- As you discuss what you'd like your ground rules to be, make sure there is consensus within the group. Everyone must agree and buy into all of them.

- When the group has reached agreement on the rules, record the final list on the "Our Group" page located on the inside back cover of this participant's guide.

Our ground rules (add your own to the list):

- Begin and end on time
- Confidentiality
- Call when you can't come
- Bring up issues or dissatisfaction right away
- No interrupting, or carrying on separate conversations

- _____

- _____

- _____

- _____

- _____

- _____

- _____

- _____

When finished, select "*Segment Two: How'd It Go?*" from the Session Three menu.

Watch this . . . 1 minute
"Segment Two: How'd It Go?"

Talk about this . . . 15 minutes

As a group, debrief your experience coming up with your ground rules. Discuss:

• What went well? What could have gone better?

• Did anyone dominate the discussion? Did anyone not participate? If so, now is the time to ask why.

When finished, select
"Segment Three: Closing Thoughts" from
the Session Three menu.

Watch this ... 2 minutes
"Segment Three: Closing Thoughts"

What we've covered ...
- Ground rules exist to guard and protect the habits so that the group process goes well

- Ground rules need to be clear and agreed upon by everyone in the group

Coming up ...
- Determining your group's structure and purpose

Close the group in prayer.

session four | determining your
group's purpose

session four | determining your group's purpose

Welcome back! Please insert DVD One and select **"Session Four: Determining Your Group's Purpose"** to begin.

Watch this. . . 15 minutes
"Segment One: Determining Your Purpose"

- It's important to determine your group's purpose

- Determining your purpose is done by answering three questions:

▶ What **kind** of group do we want to be?"

  ■ Examples:
    - Recovery group
    - Parenting group
    - Bible study
    - General growth group
    - Other

Our answer: _____

▶ What kind of **curriculum** will we use?

- Examples:
  - Bible study
  - Books
  - Curriculum provided by your church
  - Group-generated questions
  - Video/DVD curriculum
  - Other
- Regardless of the curriculum you choose, go beyond content questions and ask process questions that get at people's feelings and emotions

 Drama: Faith Asks a Process Question

- Choose course materials that fit your purpose, structure, maturity level, and interests
- Determine if the questions in the course materials will foster good discussion in the group

Our answer: _____

▶ What kind of **balance** will we have between content (facts and knowledge) and process (thoughts and feelings)?

session four | determining your group's purpose

Drama: Gregory's Small Group "Nightmares"

Our answer:

●————————————————————————————————●

Knowledge-
focused

Process-
oriented

- What will our typical **agenda** be?

  ▶ How much time will be spent on the teaching/lesson, talking and sharing, and prayer?

  ▶ Appoint a timekeeper

  ▶ Example for a 60-minute meeting:
    ■ 10 minutes of sharing
    ■ 40 minutes of interaction with the curriculum
    ■ 10 minutes of prayer

  ▶ Example for a 90-minute meeting:
    ■ 15 minutes of sharing
    ■ 60 minutes of interaction with the curriculum
    ■ 15 minutes of prayer

  ▶ Your agenda can be modified in any way to meet the needs and desires of your particular group

Our agenda:

_____

_____

_____

_____

 Talk about this . . . 25 minutes

First, pick a timekeeper. Then go back and fill in your group's answers for the questions on pages 41–42. When you have finished, record your decisions on the "Our Group" page on the inside back cover, and then select *"Segment Two: Closing Thoughts"* from the Session Four menu.

 Watch this . . . 20 minutes
"Segment Two: Closing Thoughts"

What we've covered . . .
- Connecting
- The five habits
- Ground rules
- Purpose

The purpose of small groups:
- To show grace and process truth over time
- To experience God and others

session four | determining your
group's purpose

Where do we go from here?

- DVD Two can be used two ways:
  - ▶ Use the tips in order
  - ▶ Focus on your group's highest felt needs first (see pages 46–47 to determine what they are)

When using DVD Two, remember to set aside the first 5 to 10 minutes of your meeting to watch a coaching tip and leave 5 minutes at the end to debrief what happened.

  Drama: A Snapshot of the Future

> Close the group in prayer, taking extra time to focus on the decisions you have made as a group and the new phase into which your group is about to move.

session four | determining your
group's purpose

Use the list below to identify your group's greatest felt needs.
The corresponding tip titles are on the next page. Make a
check next to the one(s) you want to start with.

Felt Needs

Care
☐ Being listened to
☐ Paying attention to group dynamics
☐ Asking "deeper" questions

Safety
☐ "Checking In": How are we really doing as a group?
☐ Identifying each other's strengths
☐ Praying as a group

Authenticity
☐ Opening up to each other
☐ Giving and getting feedback
☐ Owning your "junk" in a group

Growth
☐ Confronting others
☐ Dealing with group conflict
☐ Growing in life and spirituality

Help
☐ Helping and supporting one another in everyday life
☐ Responding to someone who's in a painful phase of life
☐ Dealing with people experiencing crisis or tragedy

Corresponding Tip Titles

Care
- ☐ Active Listening
- ☐ Being Attentive
- ☐ Asking Good Questions

Safety
- ☐ Group Check-In #1 and Group Check-In #2
- ☐ Calling Out the Best in Others
- ☐ Prayer

Authenticity
- ☐ Telling Your Story
- ☐ Giving and Receiving Feedback
- ☐ Confessing Your Faults

Growth
- ☐ When Groups Get Messy, Part 1—Confrontation
- ☐ When Groups Get Messy, Part 2—Conflict Resolution
- ☐ Helping Others Take Growth Risks

Help
- ☐ Helping and Supporting Each Other
- ☐ Responding to Someone Who Is Hurting
- ☐ Dealing with People in Crisis

ReGroup

training **groups** to be **groups**

DVD **two** participant's guide

tip one: | active listening

> Welcome back! Please insert DVD Two and select **"Tip One: Active Listening"** to begin.

Watch this . . . 7 minutes
"Tip One: Active Listening"

Definition:

Active listening is communicating to someone that you hear what they are saying so they feel heard and understood.

Biblical references:

- James 1:19— "...everyone should be quick to listen..."
- Proverbs 17:27–28— "A man of knowledge uses words with restraint."

Why it's important:

- People know they are heard and understood
- They feel valued
- They discover more about themselves
- They are known at a deeper level by others

tip one: |  active listening

How to do it:

- Make eye contact

- Listen to the person who is talking and don't interrupt

- Use statements or questions which show genuine interest and invite more communication

- Give feedback

- Not everyone in the group needs to respond verbally with questions or statements, but everyone needs to acknowledge what the person is saying (i.e., eye contact, nodding, body language)

During your group time, do this . . .

Active Listening

- Use a nonverbal active listening skill—i.e., eye contact, nodding, not interrupting, etc.

- Ask at least one follow-up question or make at least one follow-up statement that demonstrates you understand what the person is saying and that you want to know more

At the end of your group time, talk about this . . .

Take about 5 minutes to debrief as a group how it felt to actively listen and be listened to in your meeting:

- When you were talking, how did it go?
  - ▶ Did you feel understood?
  - ▶ What made you feel understood? Be specific, like "When _____ said/did _____, I felt/did not feel understood (listened to)."

- When you were listening, how did it go?
  - ▶ Did you feel comfortable asking a follow-up question? Why or why not?

Welcome back! Please insert DVD Two and select
"Tip Two: Being Attentive" to begin.

Watch this . . . 5 minutes
"Tip Two: Being Attentive"

Definition:
Being attentive is noticing and naming what is happening in both
the group process and in individuals.

Biblical references:
- Proverbs 4:1 and 5:1—God wants us to be attentive to him
- Proverbs 22:17—God wants us to be attentive to others
- Romans 12:10—We honor each other when we pay attention

Why it's important:
- Communicates love and care to those in your group
- Enables you to see where God is at work in the group
- Helps you to be aware of how people are doing in the group

tip two: | being attentive

How to do it . . .

- Pay attention to whether the following things are occurring in the group:

  ▶ Do people feel safe?

  ▶ Do they feel listened to and understood?

  ▶ Is the group asking follow-up questions?

  ▶ Is the conversation engaging? Does it flow?

  ▶ Does the group notice if someone is hurting and respond accordingly?

- When someone notices something about the group, they "name" it or mention it to the rest of the group

During your group time, do this . . .

Be Attentive

For the rest of your time together, pay attention to what's happening in the group.

Here is a reminder of the list again:

- Do people feel safe?

- Do they feel listened to and understood?

- Is the group asking follow-up questions?

- Is the conversation engaging? Does it flow?

- Does the group notice if someone is hurting and respond accordingly?

If you notice something, and it's appropriate to do so (the timing is right), "name" it for the group at that time.

Here are some examples:
- "It seems like we're spending a lot of time on this. Is there something going on or should we move on?"

- "I'm noticing that Sue shut down after that last interaction. How are you feeling, Sue?"

being attentive

At the end of your group time, talk about this . . .

Debrief how it went during your group time by answering the following questions together:

- Was being attentive difficult or easy for you? Why?

- Read the following and respond by marking an "X" on each continuum below. When you're done, share your answers with the group. Discuss why you answered the way you did.

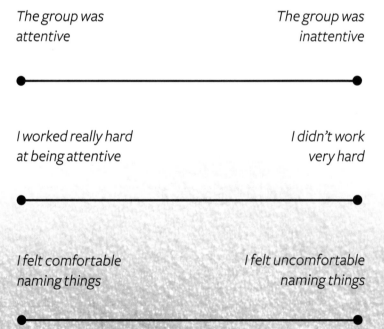

The group was
attentive

The group was
inattentive

I worked really hard
at being attentive

I didn't work
very hard

I felt comfortable
naming things

I felt uncomfortable
naming things

tip three: | telling your story (without going on and on)

> Welcome back! Please insert DVD Two and select **"Tip Three: Telling Your Story (Without Going On and On)"** to begin.

Note: You will need to set aside 15 minutes at the beginning of your meeting for this tip.

Watch this . . . 15 minutes
"Tip Three: Telling Your Story (Without Going On and On)"

Definition:
Telling your "story" means telling people about those significant events and relationships that have shaped you in the past and continue to shape you today. It includes feelings or reactions to past or present experiences.

A healthy group gives adequate time for everyone to share his or her story, but it doesn't mean everyone is going to share equally every week.

Biblical references:
- Philippians 3:1–14—Paul's story of coming to faith and his spiritual growth
- 2 Corinthians 6:11—Paul's challenge to the Corinthians to open up

tip three: telling your story
(without going on
and on)

Why it's important:
- We need to share so we'll continue to grow

- If we don't share:
  - ▸ People won't get to know one another
  - ▸ They will remain cautious
  - ▸ They'll lose interest in the group
  - ▸ The ability to grow in relationship skills will be lost

- Share your story early in the life of the group

- Real tranformation happens when our story intersects with God's story, and our story becomes like his

The two elements of sharing:
- Balance of sharing: how much each person shares
  - ▸ This must be monitored:
    - ■ "Traffic cop" method
    - ■ Structured method—assign times
    - ■ Feedback method—everyone needs to be attentive

- Quality of sharing: going deeper with each other
  - ▸ What you share—share about significant things
  - ▸ How you share—get into the vulnerability of experience

tip three: telling your story
(without going on
and on)

During your group time, do this . . .

Tell Your Story

As you meet together, be aware of the balance of sharing and choose to share on a level you haven't before. Take a bit of a risk or go one degree past your comfort zone in the sharing of your life or story.

At the end of your group time, talk about this . . .

- How was the balance of sharing in the group?
- Discuss your experience with telling your story as a group.
  - ▸ How did you take a risk?
  - ▸ What did you share?
  - ▸ How did it feel?

●————————————————————————————————●
Scary   Awkward   Safe

If you didn't share during your meeting, you may:
- Talk with the group about why it was difficult for you

- Try to share in the future after watching others do it

Welcome back! Please insert DVD Two and select
"Tip Four: Group Check-In #1" to begin.

Watch this . . . 5 minutes
"Tip Four: Group Check-In #1"

A group "check-in" is a regularly scheduled "snapshot."
It's a time at the end of a meeting (approximately 15
minutes) in which the group evaluates how things are
going according to the original goals.

Your group should do this every three to four months
(about four times a year).

group check-in #1

 At the end your group time, talk about this . . .

For this group check-in, set aside 15 minutes to answer the following questions that evaluate how your group is doing in the "truth" area. Discuss your answers together.

- How do we respond when truth is spoken?

- Does everyone feel safe to talk about their feelings?

- How well are we listening to each other?

- Are we free to say what we're thinking (even when it's a differing opinion)?

- Is there anything that needs to be said in the group that hasn't been said yet?

tip five: | asking good questions

Welcome back! Please insert DVD Two and select **"Tip Five: Asking Good Questions"** to begin.

Watch this . . . 6 minutes
"Tip Five: Asking Good Questions"

Definition:
There are two types of questions you should ask during your group meetings. They are questions that:
- Discover more information (information exchange)
- Explore experience (thoughts, feelings, etc.)

Biblical reference:
- Proverbs 20:5—"the purposes of a man's heart are deep waters and a man of understanding draws them out."

Why it's important:
- Helps you get to know the person
- Shows interest in their life
- Helps them tell their story
- Provides dialogue
- Helps the person understand themselves better

tip five: | asking good
questions

How to do it:

Examples of asking questions that . . .

- Discover more information—the facts:
  - ▶ Tell me more about that . . .
  - ▶ Where did you grow up?
  - ▶ Where do you work?

- Explore experience—thoughts and feelings:
  - ▶ What did that feel like?
  - ▶ How was your relationship with your parents?
  - ▶ How did that relationship make you feel?
  - ▶ What do you think about that?
  - ▶ What was that like for you?

| asking good
questions

 During your group time, do this . . .

Ask Good Questions

Try asking at least one information-focused and one experience-focused question during your meeting. You can choose who you want to ask, but you don't have to ask the same person each type of question.

 At the end of your group time, talk about this . . .

Looking back at your meeting . . .
- Was it easy, awkward, or hard to ask questions? Why?
- What did you notice about the group dynamic when people were intentional about asking more questions?

calling out the best in others

Welcome back! Please insert DVD Two and select **"Tip Six: Calling Out the Best in Others"** to begin.

Watch this . . . 5 minutes
"Tip Six: Calling Out the Best in Others"

Definition:

Calling out the best in others is part affirmation and part invitation—affirming something in someone and asking them to keep bringing it into the group. It applies to both individuals and to the group as a whole.

Biblical references:

- Hebrews 10:24—"Spur one another on to love and good deeds"
- Romans 12:1–8—We all have spiritual gifts that we should identify and nurture in a group context

Why it's important:

- Encourages us to be better people
- Points out places we can grow
- Helps us love other people

tip six: | calling out the best in others

How to do it:

- See it: be aware of what others are doing in the group

- Name it: name or label it clearly—be specific, give examples

- Encourage it

tip six: | calling out the best
in others

 During your group time, do this . . .

Call Out the Best in Others

Look for an opportunity—in this meeting or future meetings—to encourage at least one other person by calling out the best in them.

Examples:
- "When you pray, it seems like it really builds others up—I hope you keep doing that."

- "You are often the first person to jump in and help when the group has a need. Keep doing that, because we need it!"

- "I appreciate that you let the group know how you are really doing, even when it's painful. Keep it up."

tip six: | calling out the best
in others

 At the end of your group time, talk about this . . .

If anyone "called out the best" in someone, answer these questions:
- How did it feel to have the best called out in you?
- How did it feel to observe it?
- How did it feel to do it?
- Did you notice anything different in the group environment?

If no one did it during the group time, take time now to "call out the best" in at least one person in the group and then try to do it in future group times.

Welcome back! Please insert DVD Two and select
"Tip Seven: Giving and Receiving Feedback"
to begin.

Watch this . . . 10 minutes
"Tip Seven: Giving and Receiving Feedback"

Definition:
Giving feedback is noticing and expressing what you think, feel, or perceive about someone for their benefit and awareness. It may be positives or negatives.

Biblical references:
- Proverbs 27:5—"better is open rebuke than hidden love"
- Ecclesiastes 7:5—"It's better to heed a wise man's rebuke than listen to the song of fools"
- Colossians 3:16—". . . teach and admonish one another. . ."

tip seven: | giving and receiving
feedback

Why it's important:

- Feedback acts as a mirror—we need others to help us see ourselves and our lives accurately

- We all have blind spots, and feedback helps us to discover them

How to do it:

Giving feedback:

- Be attentive and observe each other—notice feelings, behaviors, choices, and values

- Form an understanding of what you see

- Tell the person what you see/notice and affirm them as you do so

- Tell the person why you think it's important to mention what you see

  - ▶ Have an attitude of being "for" the person

  - ▶ Use "I" statements, not "you" statements ("I see," "I notice," "I feel," "I understand," rather than "You are," "You always," etc.)

- Give the person your thoughts/opinions

giving and receiving
feedback

Receiving feedback:

- Take it in—receive it

- Sit with it

- Have an attitude that it is for you, not against you

- Ask clarifying questions (i.e., "When did you see me do this?")

- Acknowledge that you are appreciative: "thanks for telling me about that"

- Notice whether you have a tendency to be defensive or devalue the feedback

- Express emotions appropriately; avoid the following:
  ▶ Anger
  ▶ Defensiveness
  ▶ Hostility
  ▶ Stonewalling

- Don't "fake" it; instead, say something like, "This is hard to hear … I need to know you still accept and care for me after what you've said, etc."

During your group time, do this . . .

Give and Receive Feedback

Find an opportunity during this meeting or one in the near future to give feedback to someone else.

At the end of your group time, talk about this . . .

If you gave or received feedback during your meeting, what was that like for you? If no one gave feedback, as a group try to identify why.

tip eight: | helping and supporting each other

Welcome back! Please insert DVD Two and select **"Tip Eight: Helping and Supporting Each Other"** to begin.

Watch this . . . 7 minutes
"Tip Eight: Helping and Supporting Each Other"

Definition:
Helping and supporting each other is another level of the "being attentive" skill. It means providing practical help and support, including wisdom or counsel, and may occur in the group setting or outside of it.

Biblical references:
- 1 Thessalonians 5:14—Encourage the timid, help the weak
- Luke 10:25–37—The Good Samaritan

Don't give unsolicited and unwanted advice.

Help can be given inside the group context or outside the group context.

Why it's important:
- Practical ways to show the love of God
- Helps us learn how to serve

tip eight: | helping and supporting
each other

How to do it:

- Recognize what characteristics or knowledge you have that could help others in the group

- Offer to help when you see an opportunity

- Know the difference between advice and help
  - ▶ Advice = You ought to . . .
  - ▶ Helping = Can I offer . . .?

- Ask for help when you need it

At the end of your group time, do this . . .

Help and Support Each Other

In the last five minutes of the meeting:
▶ Write down one way you need help from the group below.

I need . . .

▶ Then, write down at least two ways you can offer help to the group.

I can offer . . .

1.

2.

▶ Share your answers with the rest of the group.

responding to someone who is hurting

> Welcome back! Please insert DVD Two and select **"Tip Nine: Responding to Someone Who Is Hurting"** to begin.

Watch this . . . 7 minutes

"Tip Nine: Responding to Someone Who Is Hurting"

Definition:

Responding to someone who is hurting means allowing them to express and process their pain in the context of the group.

Emotional pain is a normal part of life, and therefore a normal part of group life. It's okay to express hurt, grief, or other negative emotions, and the group needs to give permission for members to do this.

Biblical references:

- Proverbs 19:17—"He who is kind to the poor lends to the Lord"
- 1 Corinthians 12:26—When one part of us suffers, the rest of us suffer together

Why it's important:

- People feel cared about when we respond
- It presents an opportunity for growth
- We learn how to respond to others

tip nine: | responding to
someone who
is hurting

How to do it:

- Validate (identify with) an individual's pain
  - ▶ Draw out negative feelings
  - ▶ Empathize
  - ▶ Avoid:
    - ▪ Minimizing
    - ▪ Spiritualizing
    - ▪ Ignoring/denying

- Offer comfort

- Offer prayer

Before your group time, talk about this . . .

On your own, rate your group on the scale below regarding how well it does responding to people who are hurting. When everyone has finished, discuss your answers as a group.

●━━━━━━━━━━━━━━━━━━━━━━━━━━━●

Needs some
work

We're
okay

Doing
very well

As a group, discuss how your group has responded well to pain and then come up with one step to improve in this area and write it below.

Our next step:

> Welcome back! Please insert DVD Two and select
> **"Tip Ten: Helping Others Take 'Growth
> Risks'"** to begin.

 Watch this . . . 10 minutes
"Tip Ten: Helping Others Take 'Growth Risks'"

Definition:
A growth risk is any action or statement, new or out of your comfort zone, that has a possibility of a negative outcome. The challenge is given in the context of the group.

Biblical references:
- Colossians 1:28—". . . we present every person complete in Christ . . ."
- Hebrews 10:24—". . . let us consider how we may spur one another on . . ."

Why it's important:
- It's about life change
- It's not just "trying something new"—it's a real risk

tip ten: | helping others take
"growth risks"

How to do it:

- Clarify the issue

- Help people discern a next step in growth
  - ▶ Get a new job
  - ▶ Take a new course
  - ▶ Go on a date
  - ▶ Open up and share in the group

- Encourage them to take a step

- Follow up

helping others take "growth risks"

 During your group time, do this . . .

Help Each Other Take Growth Risks

Note: As a group, decide whether you want to take about 5 minutes now or to leave time at the end of the group meeting to start this activity.

Starting with this meeting, and continuing in subsequent meetings, invite two people to share a growth step and then brainstorm how the group can help them accomplish it.* Remember to discuss how your group will follow up with each other (i.e., in meetings, phone calls during the week, etc.).

Name	Growth Step	How the Group Can Help
Joe	Look for a new job	Ask about progress at each meeting

*If someone has something that's time sensitive, carve out time in the current meeting so they can share it right away.

tip eleven: | prayer

Welcome back! Please insert DVD Two and select **"Tip Eleven: Prayer"** to begin.

Watch this . . . 5 minutes
"Tip Eleven: Prayer"

Use creativity and different techniques when you pray as a group in order to expand people's understanding of what prayer can be and to deepen the connection with God and each other.

Biblical references:
- Jeremiah 29:12—"Call on me and I will answer you"
- Matthew 6:9—"Let me teach you how to pray"

Other relevant verses:
- Luke 11:2–13
- Romans 12:2
- Colossians 4:2

tip eleven: | prayer

How to do it:

Examples of kinds of prayer:
- Prayers of blessing
- Expression of sadness or frustration (lament)
- Praise
- Affirmation
- Silence
- Dedication
- Commissioning

Examples of methods of prayer:
- Small sub-groups
- Praying Scripture
- Praying through a psalm
- Prayer partners
- Quiet listening prayer
- Written prayers read out loud

Pay attention to language: avoid trite repetition or filler words (i.e., avoid "just")

During your group time, do this . . .

Pray

Experiment with a new kind of prayer during prayer time.

- Pick a kind of prayer (see list on previous page or choose your own)

- Pick a method (see list on previous page or choose your own)

- Spend a minute or two in silence

- Begin praying

If you are writing out your prayer, use the space below:

tip twelve: group check-in #2

Welcome back! Please insert DVD Two and select **"Tip Twelve: Group Check-In #2"** to begin.

Watch this . . . 5 minutes
"Tip Twelve: Group Check-In #2"

Just like a car needs a tune-up, your group needs a mid-course check-up.

Biblical references:
- 1 Corinthians 11:28—Examine yourself before coming to the Communion table
- 2 Corinthians 13:5—Examine yourselves to see whether you're in the faith

Review of grace, truth, and time:
- Grace, truth, and time are the three foundational areas of group life
- Grace = Unmerited favor
- Truth = God's truth, your truth, truth about each other
- Time = Learn, grow, and make changes

tip twelve: | group check-in #2

 During your group time, do this . . .

Check In
For this group check-in, set aside 15 minutes to answer the following questions relevant to you/your group.

To start your conversation about whether there's progress toward grace and truth (over time) in the group, decide how true the following statements are individually.

Put an "X" on the continuums where you would rate the following statements:

Group members share emotions/feelings.

More true   Less true

●——●

I think this group is a safe place.

More true   Less true

●——●

People listen to others in the group.

More true   Less true

●——●

Group members can share difficult things about their lives.

More true   Less true

●──●

People are free to express their opinions and do so.

More true   Less true

●──●

God's truth is being revealed in the group.

More true   Less true

●──●

Together, identify the area that is your group's biggest strength and the area in which you'd like to see the group grow.

If you have time, together review your group's purpose:
- Is everyone comfortable with the direction the group is going? Why or why not?

- Is there anything that you need to change?

confessing your faults

> Welcome back! Please insert DVD Two and select
> **"Tip Thirteen: Confessing Your Faults"** to begin.

Watch this ... 10 minutes
"Tip Thirteen: Confessing Your Faults"

Everyone sins or does things wrong. The group should be a safe place to talk about areas that need improvement. Talking about sin brings it out of the dark and into the light, the only place it can be healed.

Biblical references:
- James 5:16—"Confess your faults to one another so that you may be healed"
- Psalm 32:3—"When I kept silent about my sin, my bones wasted away"

tip thirteen: | confessing your faults

Points to remember:

- You may need to share differently depending on the gender mix of the group

- When to do it:
  - ▶ During personal sharing and prayer time
  - ▶ During a specific, structured time reserved for confession
  - ▶ During the process of interacting with material—"Wow, I really struggle with that."
  - ▶ As a part of prayer requests

- Express how you're feeling before you share the confession (scared, embarrassed, stupid)

- Normalize the process of confessing in the course of the discussion; when you hear someone owning a fault or weakness:
  - ▶ Don't overreact, but don't ignore it
  - ▶ Use your active listening skills (communicating to someone you hear what they are saying so they feel heard and understood; see Tip One)
  - ▶ Avoid giving advice!
  - ▶ Identify with them

During your group time, do this . . .

Confess Your Faults

You've been meeting for some time, so there should be a level of safety where there's encouragement and forgiveness from the group. When praying for each other during this group meeting, and as you feel led, name and confess some areas where you need growth or forgiveness.

If there's any relational discord, this time or after the meeting would be a good time to patch it up.

tip thirteen: | confessing your faults

 At the end of your group time, talk about this . . .

- If you took a risk and named or confessed a fault:
    - ▶ How did you feel? (scared, nervous, glad when it was over, embarrassed, safe, loved, etc.)
    - ▶ What feedback do you have for the group? What worked for you and what didn't? (i.e., "The understanding was great—I felt supported, not judged. I received a little too much advice, though. I think I just needed the group to listen.")

- Did you experience grace and truth? (i.e., support, accountability, and people who are "for" you)

when groups get messy, part 1— confrontation

Welcome back! Please insert DVD Two and select **"Extended Tip One: When Groups Get Messy, Part 1—Confrontation"** to begin.

Note: Completing this tip will take about an hour. Please plan your time accordingly.

Watch this . . . 25 minutes
"Extended Tip One: When Groups Get Messy, Part 1—Confrontation"

Definition:
Confrontation means taking feedback to the next level. It is often seen as a negative thing, but avoidance only causes more problems. The payoff is better relationships.

The word "confrontation" is not adversarial; it means to "turn your face toward" something.

Biblical references:
- Proverbs 17:10—"A rebuke impresses a person of discernment more than a hundred lashes on a fool"
- Proverbs 9:8–9—A wise person loves a rebuke
- Proverbs 29:6—"Wounds from a friend can be trusted . . ."
- Ephesians 4:25–29—Speak truth to one another

when groups get messy, part 1— confrontation

The goal is to solve issues.

People are afraid of confrontation, because they've had painful experiences with it.

Why confrontation is important:

- In some situations, if you master confrontation first, it tends to avert the need for conflict resolution

- It does two things: solves problems and creates closeness and attachment among group members

- Payoffs:
    - ▶ Promotes change in behavior
    - ▶ Promotes better relationships
    - ▶ Has a "containing" function
    - ▶ Solves problems caused by behavior that is hurting the person or hurting others
    - ▶ Promotes spiritual, relational, and emotional growth
    - ▶ Acts as a mirror for the truth
    - ▶ Promotes "wholeness"

when groups get messy, part 1— confrontation

How to do it:

- Check your attitude and motivation

- Affirm and validate the person or relationship

- State the problem and its effects; be clear and direct with specific examples

- Listen and seek to understand the response; this is a conversation

- Together, formulate solutions to the problem

Tips:

- This needs to be a dialogue

- Make an "affirmation sandwich"; don't start with the problem

- "I" language rather than "you" language: "I feel _____, when you _____"

extended tip one:

when groups get messy, part 1—confrontation

 Drama: Gregory Is Confronted, Part 1

 Talk about this . . . 5 minutes

After watching Part 1 of the drama, answer the following questions together:

- What is the issue that needs confronting?

- How would you approach the confrontation? What would you say?

> **Resume DVD**

when groups get messy, part 1— confrontation

 Drama: Gregory Is Confronted, Part 2

 Talk about this . . . 30 minutes

Now that you've seen how this group handled confrontation, think about your own skills and comfort level with this issue. Answer the following questions on your own and then share your answers with the group and discuss.

- How are you at the confronting process? Name one area you think you need to grow in so you are more effective at confrontation.

- What do you need from others when you are being confronted? (i.e., compassionate tone, "straight talk," expressions of care and acceptance, time to prepare before the conversation, etc.)

Close the group in prayer.

when groups get messy, part 2— conflict resolution

Welcome back! Please insert DVD Two and select **"Extended Tip Two: When Groups Get Messy—Conflict Resolution"** to begin.

Note: Completing this tip will take about an hour. Please plan your time accordingly.

Watch this . . . 25 minutes
"Extended Tip Two: When Groups Get Messy, Part 2—Conflict Resolution"

Drama: Conflict in the Group

Definition:
Conflict is normal! In every group, there will be people with different opinions, people who bug you, and times when you step on each other's toes. Conflict resolution is needed when two or more people contribute to a relational breakdown.

There are two types of conflict:
- Discord from disagreement, which requires resolution
- Relational breakdown, which requires reconciliation

when groups get messy, part 2— conflict resolution

Conflict shows itself in one of two ways:
- There is individual conflict within the group (two or more individuals are in conflict)

- There is group conflict—the group is divided

Why conflict resolution is important:
- Conflict takes the group off track from its mission

Biblical references:
- Ephesians 4:25—"put off falsehood and speak truthfully"
- Proverbs 19:11—"it's to a man's glory to over look an offense"
- Proverbs 18:19—" an offended brother is more unyielding than a fortified city"

- If you don't deal with conflict, it won't get resolved, and then it will destroy relationships (unity/community) or even the group itself

- Dealing with conflict is part of the life-changing power of a group; it brings a new level of honesty and safety

- Processing conflict in a healthy way is a spiritual formation process and can help in other relationships outside of the group, too

- This practice is in line with the five habits

when groups get messy, part 2— conflict resolution

How to do it:

- Check your attitude and motivation

- Affirm and validate the person or relationship

- Name reality: bring it to the person and group and say "this is my experience" and its impact; be clear and direct with specific examples (i.e., "I feel like she ran over me just now . . .")

- Allow the other party to respond

- Listen and seek to understand their response— this is a conversation

- Together, formulate a solution to the problem—find the "third place"

Tips:

- What happens in the group is dealt with in the group; follow up

- This needs to be a dialogue

- "I" language rather than "you" language: "I feel _____, when you _____"

- Ask, "What do you feel like I am not hearing?"

extended tip two:

when groups get messy, part 2— conflict resolution

Drama: The Group Resolves Its Conflict

Do this . . . 5 minutes

First, on your own, write down your answers to the following questions:

1. It bugs me when _____ happens.
   (e.g., interruptions, someone is not sensitive, we don't stop on time, someone comes in late, one person monopolizes or doesn't talk)

2. It bothers me that _____.
   (e.g., two people aren't getting along; there's tension

   between _____ and _____;

   _____ tends to judge/monopolize, etc.)

when groups get messy, part 2— conflict resolution

Talk about this . . . 30 minutes

Remembering that this is confidential information and that the goal is growth, try to work through some of these issues using the tools you have learned in this tip.

It's okay if you can't get through all or even some of your issues. Make time in your upcoming meetings to address a few of them at a time until all have been discussed.

Close the group in prayer.

dealing with people in crisis

> Welcome back! Please insert DVD Two and select **"Extended Tip Three: Dealing with People in Crisis"** to begin.

Note: Completing this tip will take about an hour. Please plan your time accordingly.

Watch this . . . 25 minutes
"Extended Tip Three: Dealing with People in Crisis"

Definition:
Responding to people in crisis or experiencing a tragedy should be done in a manner that keeps the group intact and brings resources to the person whose life is unraveling.

The group needs to know how to respond appropriately. Often the crisis will change the reality of how the group acts and interacts.

Drama: Julie's Crisis

extended tip three:

dealing with
people in
crisis

Why it's important:

- God has put your group in this person's life at this time to be his hands and feet; the group is a community and needs to show and extend compassion—that's what we're called to do

- There is no easy formula or quick fix in these situations

- The group must move toward the person, not away

Biblical references:

- Romans 15:1—"We who are strong ought to bear with the failings of the weak . . ."
- Galatians 6:2—"Carry each other's burdens . . . and thus fulfill the law of Christ"
- 1 Thessalonians 5:11—"Therefore encourage one another and build each other up"

- We are the primary resource for this person

- The severity of one person's pain affects the entire group when the individual needs long-term support

- Compassion: to suffer alongside; to come alongside one another

How to do it:

- Before the next formal meeting (during the initial hours/days of the crisis):
  - ▶ Sit and grieve with the person
  - ▶ Do any hospital visits as appropriate
  - ▶ Assign days of the week to call or visit
  - ▶ Attempt to meet any additional immediate needs that surface

- At your next formal meeting:
  - ▶ Pray with/for the person
  - ▶ Clarify the specific needs of the person
  - ▶ Determine what needs can be met both in meetings and in between meetings
  - ▶ Discuss what shifts the group needs to make in response to the new reality
  - ▶ If necessary, hold the person accountable to getting help

Tips:

- If the person cannot be in regular meetings, keep them connected to the group community
- Assess your group's agenda and put structured time in for the person to share how they are doing and/or for the group to meet their needs
- Make sure you guard the health of the group in the process

extended tip three: | dealing with
people in
crisis

Talk about this . . . 35 minutes

For this exercise, three options are outlined below and on
the next page. Read through them and decide which is most
appropriate for your group.

1. If your group has someone currently in crisis, walk through
   the steps outlined in the segment and on the previous
   page and begin to address the situation accordingly.

2. If your group doesn't have anyone in this kind of crisis
   right now, read about a real-life small group situation
   below and determine what your group would do.

*A woman in your group is going through a very volatile
divorce which involves an out-of-control spouse and
problems with her children. When she comes to group, she
is often dealing with day-to-day crises with her husband, her
kids, finances, and the legal system. She feels overwhelmed
and is often overcome with emotions to the point that she
cries for extended periods of time. Yet she wants to do the
spiritually healthy thing and remain in community, since she
desperately needs what the group offers during this time in
her life.*

dealing with people in crisis

3. If your group has faced a crisis situation in the past, think through what you did right and what you could have done differently.

Close the group in prayer.

Resources for Digging Deeper

Willow Creek Association
www.willowcreek.com/grouplife
Cloud-Townsend Resources
www.cloudtownsend.com

Theology of Community

Community 101, Gilbert Bilezikian, Zondervan, 1999. Gil was a founding elder, along with Bill Hybels and others, who helped start Willow Creek Community Church outside Chicago. This book presents the core philosophy of that church: to be the new community of God's people of faith. The book discusses what leadership and servanthood look like in community and what values make a community biblical.

Theology for the Community of God, Stanley Grenz, Eerdmans Publishing and Regent Publishing, 2000. This theological textbook develops a systematic theology using community as the organizing hermeneutic. Grenz builds this theology with the triune God at the center, highlighting God's desire to create a community for himself.

Life Together, Dietrich Bonhoeffer, Harper & Row, 1954. As a pastor in Germany under the oppressive reign of Hitler, Bonhoeffer defied the government's policy of closing churches and silencing Christian witness. As a result, he was imprisoned and later hanged, just prior to the liberation of his camp at the end of the war. During his time in confinement, he wrote *Life Together* as he learned what a community truly meant. During these months of dependence on fellow prisoners, Bonhoeffer scripted this work about the spiritual gift of communal life.

Spiritual Growth

How People Grow, Henry Cloud and John Townsend, Zondervan, 2004. People grow through relationships. As a matter of fact, lasting spiritual development is impossible to do alone. It requires people. The process involves grace and truth working in the context of relationships. The early chapters of this book describe how God administers his grace and truth through connected relationships. Later, the book details the role of acceptance, forgiveness, pain, and discipline in the spiritual growth process.

The Life You've Always Wanted, John Ortberg, Zondervan, 2002. John describes a down-to-earth process of connecting with God using a variety of spiritual practices like prayer, solitude, and reflection on Scripture to build intimacy with God.

Changes That Heal, Henry Cloud, Zondervan, 1992. Chapters One and Two describe the process of grace and truth and how they combine to produce change. The remainder of the book details how to mature into adulthood as a believer and how to bond in healthy ways with others, while learning to set boundaries to protect you from destructive habits, patterns, and relationships.

Community and Growth, Jean Vanier, Paulist Press, 1989. Vanier helped launch the L'Arche Communities, centers for the mentally disabled. While learning to shepherd and live among the disabled, he discovered the tremendous gift of community with them. Vanier, a Catholic, provides a rich inside look at the essential aspects of communal life. Non-Catholics will find some differences in theology later in the book, but most of the material focuses on shared community in Christ; Chapters One through Four are particularly helpful.

An Ordinary Day with Jesus, John Ortberg and Ruth Haley Barton, Zondervan, 2003. This DVD curriculum kit has all the resources for a class or small group to begin practicing the power of a daily connection with Jesus. Instead of limiting interaction with Christ to a morning quiet time, this resource helps you walk with Christ throughout the normal activities of your day.

The Practice of the Presence of God, Brother Lawrence, Barbour Books, 2004. This small but poignant book, a fifteenth-century classic, guides the spiritual pilgrim into seeing all of life as an opportunity for spiritual growth. Each moment, activity, and thought can become an environment for seeing Jesus at work and becoming aware of God's presence in that moment.

Building Authentic Relationships

No Perfect People Allowed, John Burke, Zondervan, 2005. As founding pastor of Gateway Community Church in Austin, Texas, Burke engages the post-modern culture by tapping into questions raised by the emerging generation. As a result of embracing the post-modern thinking at universities and in culture, people have become disillusioned and cynical about the world. Burke identifies the five key issues with which they grapple, offering an authentic, relational approach to wrestling with struggles of trust, tolerance, truth, brokenness, and aloneness. As a result, Burke has given us a great resource for connecting with people in authentic ways as they ask relevant questions about life, faith, and their role in the world. Chapters Four and Five are particularly helpful in creating an authentic environment and a "come-as-you-are" culture.

Everybody's Normal Till You Get to Know Them, John Ortberg, Zondervan, 2005. John uses his winsome approach to show how relationships are built once you get past the gleeful, false exterior we often portray. As we discover that we are all a bit broken and have quirks, the opportunity for true relationship begins to emerge.

Connecting, Larry Crabb, Word, 1997. The author describes how to create a healing community in a group. Crabb wants our souls to connect deeply; this means facing certain truths about who we are and how we connect with others—in good and bad ways. He calls us to a Spirit-inspired vision for what each person can become, a wholeness that allows them to enter into deeper relationship and growth.

The Safest Place on Earth, Larry Crab, Word, 1999. Larry focuses on creating spiritual community in the context of a group and how that community is essential to spiritual formation. Only a safe and authentic community can accomplish this.

Confrontation and Conflict
How to Have That Difficult Conversation You've Been Avoiding, Henry Cloud & John Townsend, Zondervan, 2006. Successful people confront well. They know that setting healthy boundaries improves relationships and can solve important problems. They have discovered that uncomfortable situations can be avoided or resolved through direct conversation. But most of us don't know how to have difficult conversations and see confrontation as scary or adversarial. Authors Henry Cloud and John Townsend take the principles from their bestselling book, *Boundaries,* and apply them to a variety of the most common difficult situations and relationships.

Telling Each Other the Truth, William Backus, Bethany House, 2006. If interpersonal conflict takes place between group members, this resource will help you work through it together, and guide you through a process that applies Matthew 18 in a conflict situation.

Difficult Conversations, Stone, Patton and Heen, Penguin Books, 2000. This marketplace book describes how to create a "Learning Conversation," in which you get to the root of the problem and work toward solutions and truth. The book covers topics like when to address an issue and when to let it go, what kinds of conversations work and which do not, how to really listen during a hard conversation, and the right problem-solving approach to use.

Caring Enough to Confront, David Augsburger, Regal Books, 1980. This resource describes the art of peacemaking, using a strategy of "care-fronting." The approach helps deal with anger, build trust, and handle the obstacles of blame and prejudice when working through conflict.

Connecting People into Groups

Creating Community, Andy Stanley and Bill Willits, Multnomah, 2004. If you are looking for a simple, churchwide strategy to help people in your congregation find a small group, this resource is a great starting place. Using the Northpoint Community Church as a model, the book provides a practical connection strategy that leverages the weekend service and helps guide people into deeper levels of connection and into a small group where they can grow and change.

The Seven Deadly Sins of Small Group Ministry, Bill Donahue and Russ Robinson, Zondervan, 2002. Using a diagnostic approach, this book helps church leaders to look at the small group strategy of the church through seven lenses. These include a clear ministry objective, the role of the small group point person, the shepherding structure to support leaders, leadership training and development, having a comprehensive connection strategy, using open groups to connect people, and creating a wide variety of small group opportunities. As each of the areas is diagnosed, leaders can begin to take strategic steps to remedy broken approaches and systems and develop healthy groups throughout the congregation.

Small Group Ideas and Resources

Leading Life-Changing Small Groups, Bill Donahue, Zondervan, 2002. Sections Four through Six of this essential leadership resource give leaders a vast array of ideas, events, practices, and activities for groups. Leaders always need creative ideas, and this book is filled with them.

Small Group Idea Book, Cindy Bunch, InterVarsity Press, 2003. This valuable resource provides leaders with creative ideas for connecting as a community, prayer, worship in groups, study, and outreach.

Small Group Leader Skills

Leading Life-Changing Small Groups, Bill Donahue, Zondervan, 2002. This resource is divided into eight sections. The first and last describe a structure and strategy for building and transitioning to a small group-based church. Sections Two through Seven are designed for the small group leader and provide help in the following areas: biblical leadership roles and responsibilities, personal spiritual growth habits, raising up apprentice leaders, group formation and group values, conducting life-changing meetings, group dynamics and learning styles, providing care and discipleship for members, and growing and multiplying small groups.

Walking the Small Group Tightrope, Bill Donahue and Russ Robinson, Zondervan, 2003. Russ and Bill describe the six challenges every group must navigate, including learning, development, relationships, reconciliation, impact, and connection. Included in this resource are six small group meetings with Bible study and discussion questions designed to help a group work through these challenges together.

Making Small Groups Work, Henry Cloud and John Townsend, Zondervan, 2003. John and Henry discuss how groups are essential to the process of spiritual formation. Groups become a "second family," providing discipline, care, structure, support, forgiveness, accountability, and healing. Sections cover how to start a group, the responsibilities of group facilitators, and the responsibilities of group members. Guiding group process is key—learning to listen, give feedback, name reality, provide safety, and challenge each other to grow. A final section helps groups deal with problems like needy and talkative members, passivity, and spiritualization that avoids truth.

Developing Small Group Leaders

Coaching Life-Changing Leaders, Bill Donahue and Greg Bowman, Zondervan, 2006. This resource provides a framework for supporting and developing small group leaders:

- <u>Model</u> Christlikeness and personal spiritual growth.
- <u>Guide</u> others toward growth by connecting them to resources.
- <u>Envision</u> leaders with the purpose of group ministry and their calling as shepherds and guides of others.
- <u>Equip</u> leaders with the tools and resources they need to guide a small group.

Making Small Groups Work, Henry Cloud and John Townsend, Zondervan, 2003. The section on "Responsibilities of Leaders" provides great content for training small group leaders.

Leading Life-Changing Small Groups, Bill Donahue, Zondervan, 2002. Sections on how to raise leaders for groups and within groups include apprentice development and the skills necessary for guiding a group.

Church Strategies for Group Life

Building a Church of Small Groups, Bill Donahue and Russ Robinson, Zondervan, 2001. In order to move forward with a churchwide small group ministry, church leaders should understand the theology of community, the essential components of successful group life, how to identify and develop emerging group leaders, and the key issues that must be addressed to build the ministry. Instead of teaching a specific ministry model, this book provides the tools and strategies to move forward within any model and in any kind of church.

The Seven Deadly Sins of Small Group Ministry, Bill Donahue and Russ Robinson, Zondervan, 2002. John and Henry discuss how groups are essential to the process of spiritual formation. Groups become a "second family," providing discipline, care, structure, support, forgiveness, accountability, and healing. Sections cover how to start a group, the responsibilities of group facilitators, and the responsibilities of group members. Guiding group process is key—learning to listen, give feedback, name reality, provide safety, and challenge each other to grow. A final section helps groups deal with problems like needy and talkative members, passivity, and spiritualization that avoids truth.

Personal Change and Transitions

Changes That Heal, Henry Cloud, Zondervan, 1992. Chapters One and Two describe the process of grace and truth and how they combine to produce change. In addition, the book details how to mature into adulthood as a believer and how to set boundaries to protect you from destructive habits and patterns.

Transitions, William Bridges, Addison Wesley, 1980. Bridges describes what it takes to move from an ending in life, through the "neutral zone" of ambiguity and confusion, and then into a new beginning. For people who are faced with stage-of-life changes, job losses, breakdowns in essential relationships (divorce or loss), or who simply hunger for a new pathway, this book is invaluable. Such changes require deep thought and reflection, and Bridges provides a helpful process.

Addiction and Grace, Gerald May, Harper and Row, 1988 and 2005. May has a strong grip on the power of grace to change lives and, especially, to address addictions. He argues that we are all basically addicted people and have to deal with our attachments. He provides ways to overcome our addictions and "come home" to God and authentic living.

Prayer

Waiting on God, Andrew Murray, Whitaker House, 1983. This classic has helped believers around the world for decades. Murray shares 31 meditations, one for each day of the month, guiding the reader to trust in and be renewed by Christ.

Prayer, Richard Foster, Harper San Francisco, 1992 This is a rich resource for the established believer seeking to grow in the life and practice of prayer. Many kinds of prayer practiced by saints throughout church history will challenge and refresh the reader who has settled for only one or two types of prayer.

Too Busy Not to Pray, Bill Hybels, InterVarsity Press, 1998. Bill describes a simple and effective process to learn prayer and to make it a regular part of the spiritual life. Using the acronym "ACTS," the book provides a structure to organize prayers to avoid neglecting essential aspects of prayer to God.

Using the Bible in Groups

Shaped by the Word, Robert Mulholland, Jr., Upper Room Books, 2000. Mulholland guides the reader through a process that allows a group to engage deeply with the Word. Instead of rushing to apply the text to a problem in life, he encourages the group to spend time with the author—Jesus. This method will help you understand Scripture more fully as you read it thoughtfully, ponder the meaning, listen to the voice of God as he communicates to you personally, and then discover what the text means for your growth as a community.

Spiritual Leadership

Spiritual Leadership, J. Oswald Sanders, Moody, 1994. This classic guides leaders into a process of growth. Covering prayer, family, writing, witness, character, and many other areas, this resource is a treasure of spiritual guidance and suggested practices for developing the heart of a leader.

Courageous Leadership, Bill Hybels, Zondervan, 2002. Bill shares from his many years of leading and working with leaders. This book identifies your leadership style or pathway—managerial, visionary, collaborative, and so on—and helps you thrive according to the way God designed you as a leader. Not all leaders function the same way, and this book is a great tool for discovering and using your unique style(s).

In the Company of Jesus, Bill Donahue, InterVarsity Press, 2005. This devotional is designed for leaders and seekers alike who want to connect with Jesus in Scripture and in prayer. In this way, leaders and group members can both move into a deeper relationship with Jesus. The author invites readers to encounter Jesus as provocative teacher, sacred friend, extreme forgiver, relentless lovers, truthful revealer, authentic leader, compassionate healer, and supreme conqueror.

In the Name of Jesus, Henry Nouwen, Crossroad Publishers, 1989. Nouwen gives us a great insight into the heart of spiritual leadership.

Integrity: The Courage to Meet the Demands of Reality, Henry Cloud, Harper Collins, 2006. Henry identifies six areas that must be addressed if you want the courage to face reality as a leader. These are: establishing trust, being oriented toward truth, getting results, embracing the negative, being oriented toward increase, and acknowledging transcendence.

Group Dynamics and Process

Making Small Groups Work, Henry Cloud and John Townsend, Zondervan, 2003. Cloud and Townsend provide a wealth of insight from years of working with people as Christian psychologists, especially as it relates to group life. Many groups fail for lack of understanding the processes that make them work. This book addresses how leaders and members collaborate to create an environment for spiritual growth and healing.

Safe People, Henry Cloud and John Townsend, Zondervan, 1996. This book presents a framework for discerning character, both healthy and unhealthy, in others and for how to become a safe person.

Small Group Studies

The following studies are recommended for groups that wish to integrate biblical truth with a vibrant group process. Some Bible studies are strong on content, while other studies emphasize process. Some seek to integrate both. With the hundreds of study guides on the market, we have chosen a few that illustrate integrating truth and life. Many are Willow Creek Resources we have used and proven over time. Your church leaders will also have great recommendations that honor your church's theology and emphasis. Most are designed for six sessions each, so that groups can focus for short periods of time on a given book of the Bible or issue.

Spiritual Formation Series, John Ortberg, Laurie Pederson, Judson Poling, Zondervan, 2001. This series focuses on individual and group practices as well as biblical content, so that members can practice what they are learning between meetings.

Jesus 101 Series, Bill Donahue and Keri Kent, InterVarsity Press, 2005. These guides invite participants to encounter Jesus as people of the first century did. Groups are encouraged through a process of listening, meeting Jesus in the text, joining the conversation, connecting with each other's stories, and then finding their way as a community of Jesus followers seeking to practice his way of life.

Interactions Series, Bill Hybels, Zondervan, 1999. These topical studies based on Bill's teaching are designed to engage the group on issues like character, love, authenticity, family, and other practical areas of life.

New Community Series, John Ortberg, Zondervan, 2000. Based on books of the Bible, this series invites readers to engage Scripture within the group context.

Tough Questions Series, Garry Poole, Zondervan, 2003. Garry provides wisdom from his many years of leading groups of seekers—people in the process of investigating Jesus and the claims of the Bible. Dealing with topics like "Is there a God?" and "Why is there so much suffering in the world?" groups can look at what the Bible teaches, yet have a safe place to share opinions and explore the issues.

Bible 101, Bill Donahue, Kathy Dice, Judson Poling, and Michael Redding, InterVarsity Press, 1999. This series provides a firm grip on the Bible and covers how we got the Bible, how it is organized, how to do personal Bible study, the chronology and geography of the Bible, and how to interpret the different types of Bible literature.

Just Walk Across the Room, Bill Hybels, Zondervan, 2006. For use in groups or as whole churches, this curriculum kit guides people into the adventure of simply reaching out to people we meet or work with, having conversations and exploring topics of life and faith. It is designed to promote a natural approach to starting evangelistic conversations without unnecessarily offending people.

For marriage, family, dating, and relational resources, see the Cloud-Townsend website (www.cloudtownsend.com). For other small group materials, see www.willowcreek.com, www.zondervan.com, or www.ivpress.com.

WILLOW

Willow Creek Association

Vision, Training, Resources for Prevailing Churches

This resource was created to serve you and to help you build a local church that prevails. It is just one of the many ministry tools that are a part of the Willow Creek Resources® line, published by the Willow Creek Association together with Zondervan.

The Willow Creek Association (WCA) was created in 1992 to serve a rapidly growing number of churches from across the denominational spectrum that are committed to helping unchurched people become fully-devoted followers of Christ. Membership in the WCA now numbers over 11,000 member churches worldwide from more than ninety denominations.

The Willow Creek Association links like-minded Christian leaders with each other and with strategic vision, training, and resources in order to help them build prevailing churches designed to reach their redemptive potential. Here are some of the ways the WCA does that.

- **The Leadership Summit**—a once a year, two-and-a-half day conference to envision and equip Christians with leadership gifts and responsibilities. Presented live at Willow Creek as well as via live satellite broadcast and rebroadcast events at over two hundred locations across the globe, this event is designed to increase the leadership effectiveness of pastors, ministry staff, volunteer church leaders, and Christians in the marketplace.

- **Ministry-Specific Conferences**—throughout each year the WCA hosts a variety of conferences and training events—both at Willow Creek's main campus and offsite, across the U.S., and around the world—targeting church leaders and volunteers in ministry-specific areas such as: evangelism, small groups, preaching and teaching, the arts, children, students, women, volunteers, stewardship, raising up resources, etc.

- **Willow Creek Resources®**—provides churches with trusted and field-tested ministry resources in such areas as leadership, evangelism, spiritual formation, spiritual gifts, small groups, stewardship, student ministry, children's ministry, the use of the arts—drama, media, contemporary music—and more.

- **WCA Member Benefits**—includes substantial discounts to WCA training events, a 20 percent discount on all Willow Creek Resources®, *Defining Moments* monthly audio journal for leaders, quarterly *Willow* magazine, access to a Members-Only section on WillowNet, monthly communications, and more. Member churches also receive special discounts and premier services through WCA's growing number of ministry partners—Select Service Providers—and save an average of $500 annually depending on the level of engagement.

For specific information about WCA conferences, resources, membership, and other ministry services, contact:

Willow Creek Association

P.O. Box 3188, Barrington, IL 60011-3188
Phone: 847-570-9812, Fax: 847-765-5046
www.willowcreek.com

▶▶ Walking the Small Group Tightrope:

Meeting the Challenges Every Group Faces

Bill Donahue, Russ Robinson

Leading a successful small group is like walking a tightrope — keeping the balance is the key. This book offers creative action steps and tools for addressing six distinct challenges every small group leader faces, along with clear strategies for balancing tensions in your group.

Softcover 0-310-25229-6

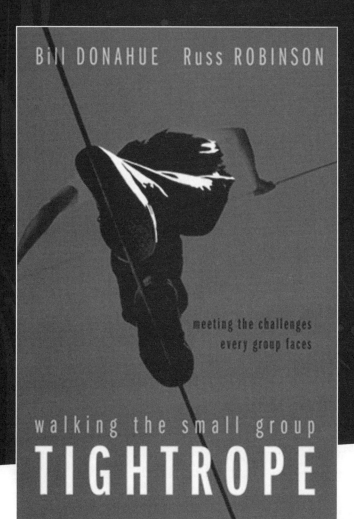

▶▶ Leading Life–Changing Small Groups, Revised:

A Comprehensive Leadership Tool for Small Group Leaders
Bill Donahue

Like nothing else, small groups have the power to change lives. This best-selling small group guidebook gives you comprehensive direction for cultivating small groups that foster discipleship and spiritual transformation. Organized in a ready-reference format, it offers a commanding grasp of topics, including group formation and values, leadership requirements and responsibilities, group structure, meeting preparation, and much more.

Softcover 0-310-24750-0

▶▶ Coaching Life–Changing Small Group Leaders:

A Practical Guide for Those Who Lead and Shepherd Small Group Leaders
Bill Donahue, Greg Bowman

Who shepherds the small group leaders who play key leadership roles in your church? This comprehensive volume details the best ways to provide support and guidance to your small group leaders, helping you model a surrendered life, find essential tools, and encourage leaders to grow spiritually.

Softcover 0-310-25179-6

WILLOW

▪ ZONDERVAN®

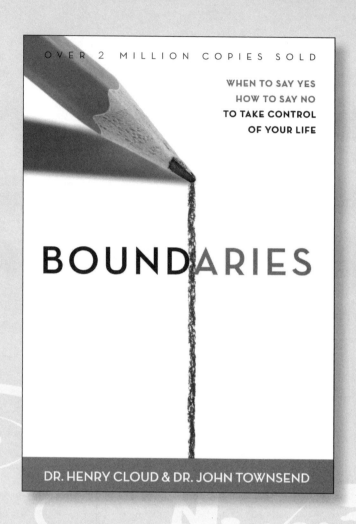

▶▶ Boundaries:

When to Say Yes, How to Say No, to Take Control of Your Life
Dr. Henry Cloud and Dr. John Townsend

Having clear boundaries is essential to a healthy, balanced lifestyle. A boundary is a personal property line that marks those things for which we are responsible. In other words, boundaries define who we are and who we are not. Boundaries impact all areas of our lives: physical boundaries help us determine who may touch us, mental boundaries give us the freedom to have our own thoughts, emotional boundaries help us to deal with our own emotions, and spiritual boundaries help us to distinguish God's will from our own.

Softcover 0-310-24745-4
DVD 0-310-27809-0
Participant's Guide 0-310-27808-2

ZONDERVAN®

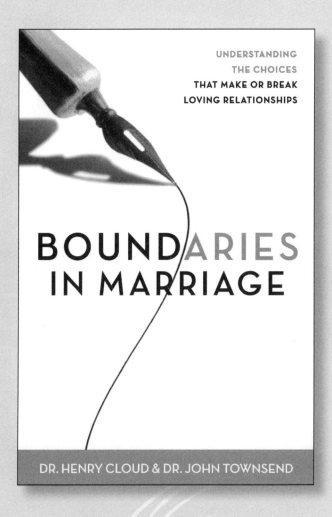

UNDERSTANDING
THE CHOICES
**THAT MAKE OR BREAK
LOVING RELATIONSHIPS**

BOUNDARIES
IN MARRIAGE

DR. HENRY CLOUD & DR. JOHN TOWNSEND

▶▶ Boundaries in Marriage

Dr. Henry Cloud and Dr. John Townsend

Learn when to say yes and when to say no—to your spouse and to others—to make the most of your marriage. Only when a husband and wife know and respect each other's needs, choices, and freedom can they give themselves freely and lovingly to one another. Boundaries are the "property lines" that define and protect husbands and wives as individuals. Once they are in place, a good marriage can become better, and a less-than-satisfying one can be saved.

Softcover 0-310-24314-9
DVD 0-310-27813-9
Participant's Guide 0-310-24615-6

ZONDERVAN®

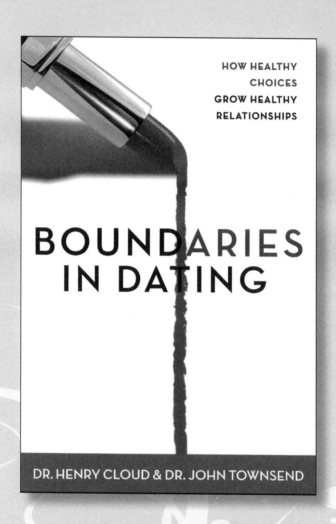

HOW HEALTHY
CHOICES
GROW HEALTHY
RELATIONSHIPS

BOUNDARIES
IN DATING

DR. HENRY CLOUD & DR. JOHN TOWNSEND

▶▶ Boundaries in Dating

Dr. Henry Cloud and Dr. John Townsend

Boundaries in Dating provides a way to think, solve problems, and enjoy the benefits of dating in the fullest way, including increasing the ability to find and commit to a marriage partner.

Softcover 0-310-20034-2

 ZONDERVAN®

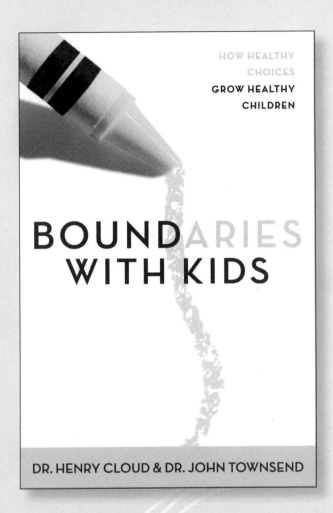

HOW HEALTHY
CHOICES
**GROW HEALTHY
CHILDREN**

BOUNDARIES
WITH KIDS

DR. HENRY CLOUD & DR. JOHN TOWNSEND

▶▶ Boundaries with Kids

Dr. Henry Cloud and Dr. John Townsend

To help their children grow into healthy adults, parents need to teach them how to take responsibility for their behavior, their values, and their lives. The authors of the Gold Medallion Award-winning book *Boundaries* bring their biblically-based principles to bear on the challenging task of child rearing, showing parents how to bring control to an out-of-control family life, how to set limits and still be loving parents, how to define legitimate boundaries for the family, and how to instill in children a godly character.

Softcover 0-310-24315-7
DVD 0-310-27811-2
Participant's Guide 0-310-24725-X

 **ZONDERVAN**®

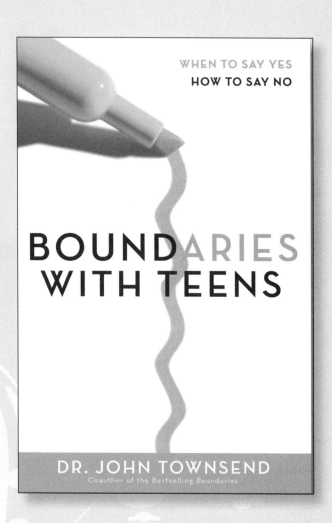

WHEN TO SAY YES
HOW TO SAY NO

BOUNDARIES
WITH TEENS

DR. JOHN TOWNSEND
Coauthor of the Bestselling Boundaries

▶▶ Boundaries with Teens
Dr. John Townsend

In this exciting new book, Dr. Townsend gives important keys for establishing healthy boundaries—the bedrock of good relationships, maturity, safety, and growth for teens and the adults in their lives. The book offers help in raising your teens to take responsibility for their actions, attitudes, and emotions.

Softcover 0-310-27045-6

 ZONDERVAN®

What we noted . . .

"Using the Five Habits" (page 26):

Care:
Faith asks Michael to talk more about why he worries.
The group listens intently when Leisha shares about her son.

Safety:
Marty takes his sunglasses off so he can make eye contact.
Kevin "breaks the ice" when no one wants to answer the first question.
Leisha puts her phone on vibrate so it won't interrupt again.

Authenticity:
Michael shares that he struggles with worry.
Leisha shares about the troubles she's having with her son.

Growth:
Marty, Gregory, and Kevin challenge Michael to talk to his boss.

Help:
Gregory, Julie, and Marty volunteer to help Michael move.

"Broken Ground Rules" (page 34):

The group doesn't begin on time.
Gregory doesn't bring up his dissatisfaction with the group.
Veronica and Julie have a conversation while Marty is trying to share.
Leisha comes in late.
Michael doesn't call when he can't come.
Faith breaks confidentiality.

authorbiographies|

Henry Cloud is a clinical psychologist, author, speaker, and cofounder of Cloud-Townsend Resources. He has written or cowritten nineteen books, including *Making Small Groups Work*. His most recent books are *How to Get a Date Worth Keeping* and *Integrity: The Courage to Meet the Demands of Reality*.

He is a graduate of Southern Methodist University, having earned a B.S. in psychology with honors. He completed his Ph.D. in clinical psychology at Biola University and his clinical internship at Los Angeles County Department of Mental Health. He lives with his wife and two daughters in Southern California.

Bill Donahue is the executive director of Group Life for the Willow Creek Association. As one of the leading voices in the small groups movement worldwide, Bill consults, teaches, and writes extensively about groups and leadership. Bill also works with the Neighborhood Life Ministry at Willow Creek Community Church. An active practitioner of leading and living in community, he is the author of many books, including *Leading Life-Changing Small Groups* and *In the Company of Jesus*, and the coauthor of *Building a Church of Small Groups, Walking the Small Group Tightrope,* and *Coaching Life-Changing Small Group Leaders*.

Bill has a Ph.D. in adult education from the University of North Texas, a master's degree in biblical studies from Dallas Seminary, and a bachelor's degree in psychology from Princeton University. Bill, his wife, and two children live in the northwest suburbs of Chicago.

John Townsend, clinical psychologist, speaker, and cofounder of Cloud-Townsend Resources, has authored or coauthored eighteen books, the most recent being *Rescue Your Love Life* and *Boundaries with Teens*. He has sold over four million copies of his books, including *Making Small Groups Work*.

Born and raised in North Carolina, Dr. Townsend earned his B.A. in psychology at North Carolina State University, graduating with honors. He went on to obtain his Master of Theology degree from Dallas Theological Seminary, again with honors, and then his master's degree and Ph.D. in clinical psychology from Biola University in California. He lives in Southern California with his wife and sons.

the five habits |

Review these five
habits often in your
group:

▶ **Care**
Being "for" each other
Encouraging each other
Coming alongside one another

▶ **Safety**
Having a "come-as-you-are" culture
Feeling safe enough to be yourself
Accepting each other unconditionally

▶ **Authenticity**
Being "real" with each other
Taking relational risks with one another

▶ **Growth**
Spurring one another on
Pushing each other to take growth steps
Naming areas where growth needs to happen

▶ **Help**
Providing resources that others may need
Asking for help when it's needed